Our Den

by Gabby Pritchard

illustrated by Alessia Girasole

CAMBRIDGE
UNIVERSITY PRESS

UCL
Institute of Education

'Look!

I've got some blankets
for the den,' said Sami.

'Good,' said Max.

'Look!

I've got some string
for the den,' said Sami.

'Good,' said Max.

'Look!

I've got some pegs
for the den,' said Sami.

'Good,' said Max.

'Look!

I've got a table
for the den,' said Sami.

'Good,' said Max.

'Look!

I've got some chairs
for the den,' said Sami.

'Good,' said Max.

'Look!

I've got some food
for the den,' said Sami.

'Good,' said Max.

'I've got a den,' said Max.

'Good,' said Sami.

Our Den ⬤ Gabby Pritchard

Reading notes written by Sue Bodman and Glen Franklin

Using this book

Developing reading comprehension

Sami and Max work together to make a den. The partnership involves Sami fetching things they need, whilst Max gives his approval to each new improvement to the den. This relationship reinforces the relative size and implied age of the two boys. The younger child is portrayed positively and he contributes usefully. The three sentence structures used in this book provide high challenge at Pink A as the reader has to be able to track left to right and return over four lines of text.

Grammar and sentence structure

- Text is well-spaced to support the development of one-to-one correspondence.
- Two to four lines of text consolidate and challenge return sweep on text with longer sentence structures.
- In contexts where children are learning English as an additional language, support by rehearsing the sentence structure orally before introducing the book.

Word meaning and spelling

- Check vocabulary predictions by attending to the first letter of nouns ('blankets', 'string', 'pegs', 'table', 'chairs' 'food').
- Reinforce recognition of frequently occurring words ('for', 'some', 'said', 'the', 'got', 'Look').

Curriculum links

Language Development – Make a class den using string, pegs and blankets, just like Sami and Max. This could be used as a reading den; children could sit on cushions to read a range of their favourite texts and maybe add some soft toys.

Develop the use of instructional language by putting children in the role of leader, providing instructions as to what to do next to form the den.

Learning Outcomes

Children can:

- understand that print carries meaning and is read from left to right, top to bottom
- use initial letter information to check understanding of picture information
- track two lines of simple repetitive text.

A guided reading lesson

Introducing the text

Give a book to each child and read the title. Discuss with the children what a den is, as some may not be familiar with the idea of building a den.

Orientation

Give a brief orientation to the text: *Sami and Max want to build a den. Sami got some things for the den. Let's see what their den looked like when they finished.*

Preparation

Page 2: *Find Sami's name. What letter did you need to look for? Find Max's name. What letter will you need to look for then?*

Sami is bringing some blankets for the den. He says 'Look. I've got some blankets for the den.' Read the line slowly enough for the children to match carefully as you read. Watch to make sure they control the return sweep when it occurs. Support and repeat if necessary. Then move to the third sentence. Say: *Max is pleased. Follow*